11+ Verbal Reasoning Practice

11+ VERBAL REASONING PRACTICE

PAMMI AND SONA THETHI

First published 2024

Copyright © Great Tutors 2024

The right of Great Tutors to be identified as the author of this work has been asserted in accordance with the Copyright, Designs & Patents Act 1988.

All rights reserved. No part of this book may be reproduced, stored in a retrieval system, or transmitted in any form or by any means, digital, electronic, electrostatic, magnetic tape, mechanical, photocopying, recording or otherwise, without the written permission of the copyright holder.

Published under licence by Brown Dog Books and The Self-Publishing Partnership Ltd, 10b Greenway Farm, Bath Rd, Wick, nr. Bath BS30 5RL, UK

www.selfpublishingpartnership.co.uk

ISBN printed book: 978-1-83952-784-5

Cover design by Kevin Rylands
Internal design by Mac Style

Printed and bound in the UK

This book is printed on FSC® certified paper

Verbal Reasoning

Verbal reasoning refers to the ability to understand and logically interpret information presented in the form of words. It involves the use of language to analyse, evaluate and draw conclusions from written or spoken information. Verbal reasoning often assesses skills such as reading comprehension, critical thinking and the ability to understand and manipulate language.

Verbal reasoning skills are important as they show a child's possible ability to learn subjects during their time at secondary school.

Practising for exams offers several benefits that can contribute to better performance and overall success. Here are some reasons why practising for exams is important:

Familiarity with Exam Format: Regular practice helps you become familiar with the format, structure and types of questions that may appear on the exam. This reduces anxiety and improves your ability to navigate the test.

Time Management: Practising exams allows you to gauge the time required for each section and question. This helps in developing effective time-management strategies during the actual exam, ensuring you can complete all sections within the allotted time.

Identifying Weaknesses: Regular practice helps you identify your strengths and weaknesses. Recognising areas where you need improvement enables you to focus your study efforts on specific topics that may be challenging for you.

Building Confidence: Repeated practice builds confidence. As you become more familiar with the material and the exam format, you gain confidence in your abilities, which can positively impact your performance on the actual exam.

Improving Recall: Practice enhances memory and recall. Repeated exposure to information reinforces learning, making it easier to remember key concepts and details during the exam.

Reducing Stress: Exam anxiety is common, but practising for exams can help alleviate stress. The more prepared you are, the more confident and less anxious you may feel when facing the actual test.

Enhancing Problem-Solving Skills: Many exams assess not only your knowledge but also your ability to apply that knowledge to solve problems. Practising different types of questions helps develop your problem-solving skills and critical thinking abilities.

Simulating Exam Conditions: Practising under conditions that simulate the actual exam environment (such as time constraints and a quiet space) helps you adapt to the test setting. This can improve your focus and performance on exam day.

Reinforcing Learning: Continuous practice reinforces what you've learned. It strengthens neural connections, making the information more accessible and easier to recall during the exam.

Tracking Progress: Regular practice allows you to track your progress over time. You can assess how well you are mastering the material and adjust your study plan accordingly.

In summary, practising for exams is a strategic approach to preparation that enhances your knowledge, skills and confidence, ultimately improving your performance on the actual test.

About Us

At the time of writing we have been tutoring for 15 years

We offer the following:

11 Plus
11 Plus tuition
Face-to-face tuition
Online tuition
Mock Exams for 11 Plus pupils
Online Mock Exams for 11 Plus pupils
Downloadable 11 Plus papers
Build-Your-Own papers for 11 Plus pupils

Secondary Schools
Secondary School tuition up to, and including, GCSE tuition
Face-to-face tuition
Online tuition
Online Mock Exams for GCSE subjects
Downloadable Mock Exams for GCSE subjects
Free exam papers (approximately 1,800 papers at the time of writing)
Free GCSE Maths worksheets
Downloadable GCSE-level papers
Build-Your-Own papers for GCSE pupils
InstaRev, a free GCSE Revision app

Contact Details
Phone: 07922 045 314
Email: support@greattutors.net

Websites
www.greattutors.net
www.instarev.co.uk

VR Exercises

11 Plus Verbal Reasoning

Type A – You have to insert a letter into the brackets in each of the questions to make four words.

e.g.   G O A ( ) A I L   :   C O A ( ) E A M

   G O A (T) A I L   :   C O A (T) E A M

The letter is **T** as it makes: GOA**T**, **T**AIL: COA**T** and **T**EAM

Now please do the following:

1) GAL ( ) AST : HOM ( ) DGE

2) WAL ( ) AME : FEE ( ) EAF

3) GAL ( ) LSO : BET ( ) WRY

4) SHO ( ) OST : TRI ( ) AIN

5) ETC ( ) ALL : EAC ( ) ILL

6) ROA ( ) AME : GOA ( ) IRE

7) LAN ( ) ASY : TIM ( ) AST

8) LEA ( ) ALL : BEE ( ) INE

9) WAL ( ) ITE : SUL ( ) ISS

10) BAL ( ) ESS : TAI ( ) AMP

11) MES ( ) AME : MIS ( ) HOP

12) HIS ( ) EAM : KI S ( ) OME

13) BES ( ) EAR : MIS ( ) YRE

14) GEA ( ) AGE : SOA ( ) ISE

15) VEA ( ) IVE : MAI ( ) ANE

16) MAN ( ) ACH : LAN ( ) AST

17) COS ( ) IME : BAI ( ) END

18) YOU ( ) IPE : NEA ( ) EAR

19) OPE ( ) EAR : MAI ( ) EON

20) TAR ( ) EAR : EAS ( ) EAM

21) STA ( ) AWN : AWA ( ) ELL

22) STA ( ) ALL : GRA ( ) EAT

23) GOA ( ) ARE : BIN ( ) EAN

24) STO ( ) INT : SLA ( ) ANE

Type B1 – Underline the odd one out from the following questions.

e.g. Cricket, football, rugby, <u>rowing</u>, basketball

The answer is **rowing** as the rest are ball games.

Now please try the following questions:

1) Earl, Lord, Dame, Viscount, Prince

2) Eight, One, Nine, Four, Sixteen

3) England, USA, France, Spain, Italy

4) Dee, Severn, Shannon, North, Thames

5) Three, Four, Two, Five, Seven

6) Madrid, Paris, Brussels, Birmingham, London

7) Lady, Earl, Countess, Princess, Dame

8) Everest, K2, Matterhorn, Victoria, Kilimanjaro

9) Seasons, Winter, Summer, Spring, Autumn

10) Months, Days, Calendar, Years, Hours

11) Nineteen, Fifteen, Seven, Two, Three

12) North, Baltic, Mediterranean, Caspian, Rhine

13) Nine, Sixteen, Twenty, Eight, Ten

14) Rhine, Seine, Volga, Atlantic, Severn

15) Danube, Seine, Eerie, Nile, Shannon

16) Arm, Leg, Nose, Ear, Torso

17) Thirty six, Twenty five, Sixteen, Fifteen, Four

18) Jenny, Billy, James, Thomas, Wendy

19) Nine, Seven, Eleven, Thirteen, Sixteen

20) Iron, Copper, Diamond, Lead, Zinc

21) Liver, Nose, Kidney, Heart, Brain

22) Train, Plane, Car, House, Ferry

23) Plane, Rocket, Horse, Hovercraft, Skateboard

24) Seven, Three, Eleven, Thirteen, Four

25) A, C, D, F, G

Type B2 – Underline the two words inside the brackets that are not related to the two words outside of the brackets.

e.g. Boat, Tug (Ocean Liner, <u>Train</u>, Submarine, Yacht, <u>Car</u>)

The answer is **train** and **car** as the others are water-based forms of transport.

1) Earl, Prince (Countess, Viscount, Dame, Lord, King)

2) Princess, Queen (Baron, Countess, Lady, Earl, Empress)

3) Jupiter, Mars (Saturn, Neptune, Mercury, Sun, Universe)

4) Cow, Dog (Cat, Monkey, Wolf, Ape, Elephant)

5) Chess, Draughts (Backgammon, Hockey, Ludo, Swimming, Snakes & Ladders)

6) Hour, Second (Time, Minute, Month, Year, Measurement)

7) Tuba, Clarinet (Saxophone, Piano, Violin, Trumpet, Trombone)

8) Table, Ben Nevis (K2, Matterhorn, Serengeti, Yosemite, Kilimanjaro)

9) One, Three (Nine, Four, Eleven, Six, Fifteen)

10) England, France (Argentina, Spain, Italy, Brazil, Greece)

11) Bristol, Leeds (Brighton, Warsaw, Berlin, Blackpool, Liverpool)

12) Paris, London (Leeds, Warsaw, Rome, Prague, Nice)

13) Diamond, Ruby (Brass, Diamante, Emerald, Sapphire, Opal)

14) Ballet, Hip-Hop (Maypole, Walking, Jitterbug, Running, Waltz)

15) Four, Nine (One, Two, Nine, Sixteen, Twelve)

16) Spice Girls, Beatles (Justin Bieber, Take That, Girls Aloud, Westlife, Michael Bublé)

17) Seven, Three (Four, Twenty One, One, Five, Eleven)

18) Mozart, Beethoven (Schubert, Verdi, Seal, Madonna, Brahms)

19) Two, Four (Five, Six, Seven, Eight, Ten)

20) Happy, Content (Elated, Anxious, Ecstatic, Pleased, Morose)

Type C

A B C D E F G H I J K L M N O P Q R S T U V W X Y Z

e.g. if **E B S L** means **D A R K**, what is the code for **B E L T**?

The answer is: **C F M U** – the code, in this case, is always the next consecutive letter in the alphabet.

Please do the following:

1) If F E H F means E D G E, what does S F T U mean?

2) If 20 18 1 9 14 means T R A I N, what does 22 15 9 3 5 mean?

3) If G P F K P I means E N D I N G, what does R C U V C mean?

4) If D Q O H means C O L D, what does L K V W mean?

5) If G 15 T R 5 means H O U S E, what does S Z 2 12 D mean?

6) If Q P U V means T U B E, what is the code for T I C K ?

7) If N D B M means M E A N, what is the code for Q U E E N ?

8) If D S S O H means A P P L E, what is the code for T O W E R ?

9) If 19 20 5 5 12 means S T E E L, what is the code for D A N G E R ?

8   11+ Verbal Reasoning Practice

10) If Q M X C S means P O W E R, what is the code for F L I G H T?

11) If 5 13 25 10 means G O A L, what is the code for H E L P?

12) If I N U D M means H O T E L, what is the code for T R U S T?

13) If the code for S M I L E is 21 15 11 14 7, what is the code for T R A I L?

14) If the code for H O V E R is 8 14 22 4 18, what is the code for T I M I D?

15) If the code for C L O W N is A 14 M 25 L, what is the code for H O R S E?

16) If the code for S E V E N is T C W C O, what is the code for L O D G E?

17) If Q M S A M is the code for R O V E R, what does the code S P X E I mean?

18) If Q M Z A W is the code for P O W E R, what does the code N M D J mean?

19) If S I D Z H is the code for P L A C E, what does the code C B E O D mean?

20) If G J B E S A is the code for F L Y I N G, what does the code U M D O Y mean?

The word **S U B S T A N T I A T E** is written as @ # - @ + & ! + = & + \

What is the code for the following words?

1) S T A T E   @ + & + \

2) S T U B   @ + # -

3) A B A T E   & - & + \

4) A N T E N N A E   & ! + \ ! ! & \

5) S U B S T I T U T E   @ # - @ + = + # + \

D A N G E R O U S is written as @ # - + & ! = \ $

What is the code for the following words?

6) G R A N D   + ! & ! @

7) R O A D S   ! = & @ $

8) R A N G E R   ! # - + & !

9) R E G A R D   ! & + # ! @

10) G R O U N D S   + ! = \ - @ $

T E M P E R A T U R E S is written as @ # - + # \ / @ = \ # !

What is the word for the following codes?

11) @ \ / - + !   TRAMPS

12) @ \ = - + # @   TRUMPET

13) \ # + # / @   REPEAT

10   11+ Verbal Reasoning Practice

14) ! @ \ # # @ !   _____

15) + \ # - / @ = \ #   _____

T R E M E N D O U S is written as @ # - + - \ / = ! &

What is the word for the following codes?

16) / # = \ - &   __DRONES__

17) + - \ / - /   __MENDED__

18) / - + = \ &   __DEMONS__

19) + = / - # \   __MODERN__

20) @ # ! & @   __TRUST__

Code H G F K V M W L F H means S T U P E N D O U S.

Use the same code to work out the code for the following:

21) S T U N   (H G F M)

22) P E N D   (K V M W)

23) P E N T   (K V M G)

24) S O U P   (H L F K)

25) D E N T   (W V M G)

Code G V O V E R H R L M means T E L E V I S I O N

Use the same code to work out the code for the following:

26) N E S T (   )

27) N O S E (   )

28) T O N E (   )

29) V E S T (   )

Code C O K C D N G means A M I A B L E

Use the same code to work out the code for the following:

30) A B L E (   )

31) B A L E (   )

32) M A L E (   )

33) B E A M (   )

Code Z I L S B O A means C L O V E R S

Use the same code to work out the WORD for the following:

34) L O V E (   )

35) R O V E (   )

36) L O S E (   )

37) C O V E (   )

12   11+ Verbal Reasoning Practice

Code E K T V B P D G means D I S T A N C E

Use the same code to work out the WORD for the following:

38) S T A N D   (T V B P E)

39) T E N D   (V G P E)

40) S A N D   (T B P E)

41) D A N C E   (E B P D G)

42) S T A N C E   (T V B P D G)

Type D - Underline one word from each group that are the most similar.

e.g. (twisted, surprised, <u>plain</u>) : (unusual, <u>simple</u>, flounder)

The two most similar words are **plain** and **simple**.

1) (happy, smiling, pleased) : (displeased, content, smug)

2) (marathon, lonely, tired) : (fatigued, anxious, worried)

3) (excellent, kind, assertive) : (miserly, thorough, forceful)

4) (dullard, clever, mundane) : (intelligent, strong, brave)

5) (considerate, curious, capable) : (disable, thoughtful, weird)

6) (twist, reluctance, hindrance) : (obstruction, tepid, tardy)

7) (dull, dismal, placid) : (understand, calm, noisy)

8) (dogged, dreary, hard) : (determined, clever, insightful)

9) (comprehend, confuse, ignorant) : (miniscule, tired, understand)

10) (average, tapered, broad) : (wide, slim, trim)

11) (indolent, boisterous, industrious) : (unhappy, tired, lazy)

12) (reduce, increase, unchanged) : (gain, get, fetch)

13) (ingest, digress, redress) : (address, swallow, reduce)

14) (diet, consume, eject) : (eat, basic, complex)

15) (chat, shout, whisper) : (discard, lose, converse)

16) (fascinated, neutral, distracted) : (helpful, riveted, rude)

17) (trust, discord, trial)   :   (disagreement, offense, leverage)

18) (trivial, tirade, touch)   :   (messy, helpful, unimportant)

19) (mindful, mundane, miser)   :   (boring, exciting, interesting)

20) (normal, standard, unusual)   :   (obvious, original, odd)

21) (tangible, retarded, reverse)   :   (forward, wise, real)

22) (simple, belief, flourish)   :   (faith, complex, flower)

Type E – Find a hidden four-letter word. It will span two words, or three, words

e.g. 'hi**s and** her' would produce **sand** as the four-letter word.

Please do the following:

1) I crossed the bridge with Ann holding my hand

2) In chess, some attacks are more dangerous than others

3) My best holiday was when we climbed Gerhill Hill

4) Two odious characters knocked on my door yesterday

5) Whenever she drank a soda she felt very happy

6) The plane flew over the clouds because of the thunderstorm

7) Chess is the best game ever according to Neil

8) Who lives in a yellow and green house in Spain?

9) Poker is a game played for money by gamblers

10) I like to drink at least two cups of tea a day except on the USA's Independence Day

11) Giant apes once ruled this planet

12) I go swimming three days a week

13) The problem with islands is that they are surrounded by water

14) Messing about in quicksand is never your best choice for a hobby

15) There are no more cakes left

16) The cupboard contains twenty reams of printer paper

17) The sheriff strode through the bar door

18) I want you to listen to the gurgle of the stream

19) Their shirts were always dirty and smelly

20) Half a day is less than one whole day

11 Plus Verbal Reasoning   17

Type F – Three consecutive letters are missing from one of the words in each of the sentences below. The three letters should make a word – you should not re-arrange the three letters to make the word. Write the three letter word in the brackets.

e.g. I was three HS late for school today. (our) : In this example HS becomes h**our**s

Please do the following:

1) Fir trees are ALS green.   (   )

2) I think there are eight PLAS in our Solar System.   (   )

3) SARES are my favourite type of fish to eat.   (   )

4) A lot of people like to go BING on the lake.   (   )

5) Great Whites and Hammerheads are type of SHS   (   )

6) GUIS are very popular musical instruments.   (   )

7) If you always tell the truth, people will BEVE you (   )

8) Where is the NEST train station please?   (   )

9) I think that it's CER in Winter than in Summer.   (   )

10) GEMSTS are used in a lot of jewellery.   (   )

11) Every wife has a HUSD.   (   )

12) You should be CFUL when crossing a busy road. (   )

13) BIRMING is a major UK city.   (   )

14) Get your HCUT, you long-haired hooligan!   (   )

15) Horses can CER as well as gallop. (   )

16) I'm MEEG my friend in the park in 5 minutes. (   )

17) COMERS are very fast at processing information (   )

18) All Maths questions should be really SLE. (   )

19) These servicemen are usually known as SIERS (   )

20) Keep all perishable food items in the FGE. (   )

21) Some athletes are good at THING the javelin. (   )

Type G - In the following questions, give your answer either as a number (N) or a letter (L):

e.g. (3B + C) ÷ A   (N)

The answer is (3 x 2 + 5) ÷ 1 = 11 [because the answer should be a **N**umber (N)]

A = 1, B = 2, C = 5, D = 7, E = 10

Letter (L) or Number (N)

1) A + B + C =   (N)

2) C − 2B =   (L)

3) A + B + D =   (L)

4) E ÷ C + A =   (N)

5) 2A + E ÷ B =   (L)

A = 3, B = 2, C = 12, D = 6, E = 5

6) C ÷ D =   (L)

7) B + 2A + C =   (N)

8) 4A ÷ D =   (L)

9) (A + C) ÷ E =   (L)

10) (C + D) ÷ (A x B) =   (L)

A = 10, B = 7, C = 3, D = 2, E = 4

11) (A + D) ÷ (E + D) =   (L)

12) (B + C) ÷ A =   (N)

13) (5E) ÷ (2D) =   (N)

14) A − B =   (L)

15) (A + B + C) ÷ E =   (N)

A = 4, B = 5, C = 6, D = 9, E = 11

16) (D + E) ÷ A =   (L)

17) D ÷ C + B =   (N)

18) E x C + A =   (N)

19) B + C − E =   (N)

20) D + C − A =   (L)

Type H – Underline one word from each group that are most opposite in meaning.

e.g. (<u>willing</u> / anxious / placid) :   (simpleton / cautious / <u>reluctant</u>)

Willing and **Reluctant** are the two most opposite words from the two groups.

Now please do the following:

1) (happy / concerned / confused)   :   (excited / sad / worried)

2) (timid / placid / tired)   :   (flustered / miserable / tired)

3) (hoarse / sparse / fat)   :   (thin / calm / wavy)

4) (huge / enormous / tall)   :   (wary / interested / short)

5) (dark / damp / dusty)   :   (hot / light / doubtful)

6) (evening / day / week)   :   (month / morning / year)

7) (content / unaware / timid)   :   (unhappy / shy / ignorant)

8) (ancient / ancestor / old)   :   (adult / young / toddler)

9) (dark / light / full)   :   (wait / weight / heavy)

10) (flexible / stiff / tight)   :   (rigid / round / square)

11) (enthusiastic / keen / energetic)   :   (effervescent / lethargic / unhappy)

12) (tense / brief / quiet)   :   (allow / intermittent / slack)

13) (quiet / quite / quick)   :   (fast / loud / slacken)

14) (clear / wise / true)   :   (weird / hazy / time)

15) (tougher / beaten / soften)   :   (harden / younger / gracious)

16) (tepid / boiling / warm)   :   (cold / frigid / freezing)

17) (increased / widened / doubled) :   (tripled / reduced / constant)

18) (indifferent / troubled / frowning) : (smiling / poker-faced / depressed)

19) (continuous / elevated / declined) :   (bemused / reduced / accepted)

20) (introvert / friendly / helpful) :   (extrovert / subdued / indifferent)

21) (vertigo / anorexic / charming) :   (willing / obnoxious / wary)

Type I – Use three of the numbers on the left-hand side of the colon to make the equation on the right correct.

e.g. 1 2 3 4 5 : 22 = (5 x 4 + 2)

Now do the following:

1) 3 4 7 10 20 : 12 = (÷   +   )

2) 1 3 5 6 7 : 13 = (X   −   )

3) 2 4 6 9 14 : 5 = (+   ÷   )

4) 2 3 7 8 10 : 15 = (÷   X   )

5) 1 4 7 8 9 : 65 = (X   −   )

6) 2 3 18 20 40 : 17 = (÷   −   )

7) 3 5 7 9 81 : 20 = (÷   −   )

8) 1 3 5 8 9 : 16 = (+   −   )

9) 1 3 6 7 10 : 23 = (+   +   )

10) 2 4 5 6 12 : 66 = (X   +   )

11) 1 3 4 7 9 : 23 = (X   −   )

12) 2 3 5 6 7 : 7 = (÷   +   )

13) 3 5 6 8 10 : 86 = (+   X   )

14) 2 4 7 8 11 : 1 = (−   −   )

15) 1 5 7 12 13 : 103 = (X   +   )

16) 2 3 5 6 7   :   10 = (÷   X   )

17) 2 3 5 7 9   :   21 = (÷   X   )

18) 4 5 6 7 8   :   28 = (−   X   )

19) 2 4 5 11 13   :   68 = (X   +   )

20) 1 4 7 8 9   :   14 = (÷   X   )

Type J – Move a letter from the first word to the second to make two new words.

e.g. RIDER and BAT become (_RIDE_) and (_BRAT_)

1) LEVER and HALE   become   (   ) and (   )

2) SPACE and TOOL   become   (   ) and (   )

3) COLD and MET   become   (   ) and (   )

4) MILD and KIN   become   (   ) and (   )

5) BRAIN and ANT   become   (   ) and (   )

6) ABLE and RAIN   become   (   ) and (   )

7) COMB and OAT   become   (   ) and (   )

8) DART and ICE   become   (   ) and (   )

9) CROW and BAN   become   (   ) and (   )

10) MAST and NET   become   (   ) and (   )

11) STOW and PAR   become   (   ) and (   )

12) REAP and PER   become   (   ) and (   )

13) HASTE and TRAP   become   (   ) and (   )

14) HOUSE and POT   become   (   ) and (   )

15) CRASH and WITH   become   (   ) and (   )

16) RATE and PAL   become   (   ) and (   )

17) DRONE and CAT   become   (   ) and (   )

18) TAINT and WIT   become   (   ) and (   )

19) DOLE and PANE   become   (   ) and (   )

20) MOAT and LAD   become   (   ) and (   )

26   11+ Verbal Reasoning Practice

Type K – Work out the rule used in the sequence for the first two sets of numbers and apply the rule to the third set of numbers. Write the number missing from the brackets.

e.g. 2 (8) 10 : 18 ( ) 28 : 5 ( ) 12

In the first set of numbers, or 10 – 2 = 8

In the second set the missing number is 28 – 18 = 10

The answer is 12 – 5 = 7

Please do the following:

1) 3 (13) 8   :   2 (16) 9   :   5 (   ) 5

2) 10 (27) 7   :   16 (52) 20   :   12 (   ) 9

3) 11 (20) 29   :   15 (16.5) 18 :   8 (   ) 28

4) 3 (36) 11   :   17 (44) 9   :   13 (   ) 6

5) 5 (31) 6   :   9 (93) 12   :   10 (   ) 4

6) 10 (20) 20   :   4 (13) 18   :   7 (   ) 22

7) 6 (10) 16   :   7 (12) 25   :   9 (   ) 64

8) 12 (64) 20   :   5 (36) 13   :   11 (   ) 21

9) 36 (4) 9   :   20 (2) 10   :   72 (   ) 9

10) 20 (28) 12   :   19 (35) 3   :   13 (   ) 6

11) 7 (17) 27   :   23 (29.5) 36 :   100 (   ) 4

12) 6 (30) 3   :   7 (39) 5   :   10 (   ) 8

13) 14 (44) 15 : 9 (25) 8 : 4 ( ) 13

14) 10 (5) 4 : 8 (2) 8 : 9 ( ) 9

15) 4 (20) 4 : 5 (149) 12 : 14 ( ) 8

16) 9 (0) 3 : 15 (3) 4 : 30 ( ) 6

17) 5 (23) 8 : 9 (38) 19 : 17 ( ) 6

18) 6 (10) 8 : 11 (15) 13 : 7 ( ) 9

19) 11 (9.5) 8 : 6 (33) 60 : 20 ( ) 4

20) 1 (65) 8 : 7 (56) 7 : 5 ( ) 6

Type L – A B C D E F G H I J K L M N O P Q R S T U V W X Y Z

Use the alphabet above to help work out which two letters come next in the following sequences.

e.g. Z Y X W V __U__ __T__

The sequence, in this case, is reading the alphabet backwards.

Please do the following:

1) A C E G I   ____ ____

2) Z W T Q N   ____ ____

3) B Z X V T   ____ ____

4) D F I M R   ____ ____

5) P N K G B   ____ ____

6) M O N P O   ____ ____

7) E J O T Y   ____ ____

8) Z A X C V   ____ ____

9) A Z C X E   ____ ____

10) A B D G K   ____ ____

11) Z Y W T P   ____ ____

12) E J G L I   ____ ____

13) Y T V Q S   ____ ____

14) B D Z B X   ____ ____

15) W Z V Y U   ____ ____

16) B E G K M   ____ ____

17) W S Q M K   ____ ____

18) A B C E H   ____ ____

Type M – Find the two words, one from each group that will complete the sentence most accurately. Underline both words.

e.g. Dog is to (one, two, <u>four</u>) as ape is to (three, <u>two</u>, four)

A dog has four legs and an ape has two legs.

1) Driver is to (bike, car, skateboard) as pilot is to (plane, train, go-kart)

2) Pane is to (door, roof, window) as mattress is to (bed, sofa, chair)

3) Carpet is to (bed, floor, kitchen) as grass is to (shed, rake, meadow)

4) Bullet is to (gun, fork, helmet) as arrow is to (bow, javelin, catapult)

5) Cheese is to (bread, milk, jam) as bread is to (toast, sandwich, wheat)

6) Beef is to (dog, horse, cow) as pork is to (pig, goat, chicken)

7) Lamb is to (horse, sheep, goat) as kid is to (cow, zebra, goat)

8) Ball is to (archery, horse-riding, cricket) as stick is to (rugby, hockey, tennis)

9) Fish is to (sea, land, sky) as bird is to (sky, land, sea)

10) Lion is to (sand, land, safe) as trout is to (water, tree, salt)

11) Train is to (time, city, rail) as car is to (river, rail, road)

12) Petrol is to (fuel, car, train) as bread is to (brown, white, food)

13) Amazon is to (Europe, Asia, South America) as Nile is to (Africa, Asia, Europe)

14) Himalayas is to (mountain range, climbing, Everest) as Pacific is to (sea, ocean, river)

15) Alphabet is to (seeing, words, listening) as numbers are to (arithmetic, exams, test)

16) Carnivore is to (jungle, meat, food) as Herbivore is to (vegetables, forest, diet)

17) Silver is to (gold, necklace, metal) as ruby is to (liquid, stone, gas)

18) Australia is to (country, state, town) as London is to (country, continent, city)

19) Molar is to (stomach, eye, tooth) as Iris is to (eye, ear, arm)

20) Thermometer is to (disease, temperature, fever) as ruler is to (centimetres, length, millimetres)

21) Sunrise is to (East, light, warmth) as sunset is to (cold, lights, West)

22) Triangle is to (four, three, five) as pentagon is to (seven, six, five)

23) Farming is to (wheat, rice, agricultural) as manufacturing is to (industrial, cars, toys)

Type N – Four of the five words are written in code. One of the words has not been given as a code. The codes have not been written in the same order as the words.

Answer the questions below.

PINE CAPS SPIN NICE SCAN

8953 2983 5421 1548

1) SPACES ___ 124531

2) PENANCE ___ 2384853

3) 54831 ___ CANES

4) 248951 ___ PANICS

SEER RIPE TIME SITE RISE

2947 3772 3957 5987

5) PERT ___ 4725

6) PRIM ___ 4298

7) MESS ___ 8733

8) 3927 ___ SIRE

PORE REAP REAR TEAR PARE

5673 8675 3756 3456

9) PEAT ___ 3678

10) TAPE ___ 8736

11) 5 4 3 6 _____

12) 7 5 6 7 _____

NOTE   SEND   TEST   TONE   NEST

6 5 3 4   3 4 1 3   3 5 6 4   1 4 6 2

13) D E N T _____

14) D O N E _____

15) 1 4 4 6 _____

16) 3 4 6 2 _____

PAST   TEAM   MEAT   SEEP   MAST

1 5 2 3   3 4 5 6   6 4 5 3   2 4 4 1

17) P E S T _____

18) T A M E _____

19) 2 5 6 4 _____

20) 2 4 5 3 _____

REST   SITE   REAR   AREA   TEAR

6 4 5 3   4 2 3 5   6 5 1 6   3 5 1 6

21) R A T E _____

22) S E A T _____

23) 3 5 1 4 5 _____

24) 3 6 5 5 4 _____

Type O – Apply the rule used in the first two sets of words to the third set.

e.g. shame, ham / toned, one / smiles, _____

The word is **mile** as the first and last letter have been removed.

Please do the following:

1) bread, read / small, mall / pearl, _____

2) dread, read / gripe, ripe / swish, _____

3) hard, had / bard, bad / pail, _____

4) trump, bump / treat, beat / sweet, _____

5) home, hoe / tome, toe / pawn, _____

6) twin, win / spin, pin / town _____

7) stow, tows / slay, lays / speck, _____

8) ware, water / care, cater / pare, _____

9) palace, pale / manage, mane / tonnage, _____

10) house, hue / goats, gas / smart, _____

11) timid, mid / staid, aid / strut, _____

12) canter, tan / canvas, van / manmade, _____

13) mind, mine / hale, half / pass, _____

14) inlaid, id / instant, it / tempo, _____

15) print, pray / trail, tray / slowly, _____

16) spinner, sin / planning, pan / grotesque, _____

17) haste, hate / paint, pant / grain, _____

18) sight, site / paint, pate / knave, _____

Type P – Work out the rule used in the sequence and apply it to the missing number – write the number in the space provided.

1) 1 3 5 7 _____

2) 2 4 8 16 _____

3) 240 _____ 60 30 15

4) 3 9 _____ 81 243

5) _____ 5 8 13 21

6) 1 4 9 _____ 25

7) 2.5 4.0 5.5 7.0 _____

8) 3.25 3.50 3.75 _____ 4.25

9) 12.70 _____ 11.70 11.20 10.70

10) 144 121 _____ 81 64

11) _____ -8 -12 -17 -23

12) 77 72 66 59 _____

13) 3 9 27 81 243 _____

14) 18 _____ 21 28 24

15) 100 80 90 70 _____

16) 25 _____ 5 500 1 2500

17) 1 2 4 7 11 _____

18) 24 23 _____ 18 14 9

19) 3 5 4 _____ 5 7

20) _____ 97 98 96 97 95

21) 4 _____ 64 256 1024 4096

22) 3125 625 _____ 25 5 1

23) 8 5 _____ -1 -4 -7

24) -13 _____ -8 -4 1

25) -2.8 -2.5 -2.2 -1.9 -1.6 _____

26) -12.5 -12.25 -12.0 -11.75 _____ -11.25

27) 900 _____ 600 450 300 150

28) 2 6 18 _____ 162 486

29) 486 162 54 18 6 _____

30) 1200 _____ 1050 1025 900 875

Type Q – Combine one of the words from the group on the left with a word from the right group to make a word. Underline the two words combined.

e.g. tea / coffee / <u>house</u> : car / <u>hold</u> / train (makes **household**)

Please do the following:

1) bee / be / let : small / hive / damp

2) cat / car / can : ten / wet / pet

3) foot / mouth / house : some / news / ball

4) to / hand / met : some / net / crate

5) in / new / put : teen / let / pipe

6) tall / pat / cross : tern / house / flat

7) lab / call / deep : turn / ball / our

8) view / trip / can : loot / did / hour

9) bat / ball / glove : on / our / over

10) mouse / home / to : game / clap / trap

11) over / mine / hand : trip / turn / tyre

12) ocean / river / sea : ten / hen / son

13) cross / same / son : bow / dam / dumb

14) safe / soft / sun : burn / ten / ton

15) cat / hall / net : call / small / ball

16) goal / save / catch : it / post / lost

17) set / orb / view : set / it / bet

18) flow / farm / form : seam / some / hand

19) mend / vet / ab : new / tray / cess

20) be / sound / can : hard / little / tree

Type R – **In each question below, the three words in the second group should go together in the same way as the three in the first group. Work out the word missing in the second group and write it in the brackets.**

e.g. D A M P (A M E N) T E N T : G L I B (L I A R) W A R P

1) D U K E (D U S T) M O S T   :   B A N K (   ) W A I T

2) E L S E (L O V E) V O I D   :   E A S Y (   ) A W R Y

3) M O S T (H O M E) H A R E   :   S E E P (   ) P A R T

4) T A R T (T A L E) A B L E   :   M E L T (   ) B E A N

5) T U B E (B O A T) G O A L   :   T O N E (   ) S E A M

6) T O I L (T R I M) D R U M   :   P O L E (   ) H E A T

7) G R I D (P R O D) P O O L   :   G A T E (   ) S T E M

8) S A L T (S I T E) K I T E   :   T E A M (   ) Z O N E

9) C O N E (C A R E) B R A T   :   P A L E (   ) D R A Y

10) M E A T (D I M E) D I R T   :   A L S O (   ) G O A D

11) F A C E (F A M E) T I M E   :   B O L D (   ) G O N E

12) D O U R (P R O D) T R A P   :   E L A N (   ) S O A P

13) C R A B (C L A P) P O L E   :   D O M E (   ) P E A T

14) M I S T (S O M E) B O N E   :   M O T H (   ) L I K E

15) P E S T (T E S T) T O R T   :   M O A T (   ) C E L L

16) B I L E (G L I B) G O A L   :   R A I D (   ) B O R E

17) H A T E (H O P E) P O S T   :   S O A R (   ) A C H E

18) C O A T (T A P E) P E A T   :   H A R P (   ) O P E N

19) C A R T (C U R E) L U T E   :   S U N K (   ) W E L D

20) M O R E (H A R M) A C H E   :   R E A M (   ) E L S E

21) R A I L (P E A R) P E S T   :   E T O N (   ) L A R D

22) P U N T (P U R E) R E S T   :   D R I P (   ) A W A Y

23) G U S T (T O U R) D O O R   :   S L A M (   ) W I L D

Type S1 – The three words outside the brackets are connected to two words inside. Underline the two words inside the brackets.

e.g. Saturn, Jupiter, Venus (Sun, star, <u>Earth</u>, <u>Mars</u>, asteroid) : (They are all planets.)

Please do the following:

1) lead, silver, copper (brass, gold, plastic, glass, platinum)

2) day, nanosecond, minute (second, calendar, hour, time, night)

3) rugby, cricket, tennis (swimming, running, football, netball, archery)

4) London, Paris, Madrid (Rome, Naples, Denver, Los Angeles, Moscow)

5) USA, France, Japan (Leeds, Leicester, Italy, Romania, Belgrade)

6) Thames, Rhine, Seine (Volga, Michigan, Superior, Danube, Eerie)

7) Kent, Sussex, Surrey (Bristol, Yorkshire, Lancashire, Brighton, Manchester)

8) Leeds, Liverpool, London (York, Birmingham, Leicester, Loughborough, Sheffield)

9) Everest, Ben Nevis, Mont Blanc (Andes, Matterhorn, K2, Superior, Himalayas)

10) five, seven, three (four, two, six, eleven, ten)

11) saxophone, tuba, French horn, (piano, trumpet, viola, flute, violin)

12) sixteen, twenty five, nine (four, seven, one, ten, eleven)

13) chrysanthemum, rose, orchid (poplar, iris, petunia, redwood, pampas)

14) bee, fly, midge (koala, wasp, locust, worm, dog)

15) square, rectangle, rhombus (parallelogram, triangle, circle, trapezium, oblong)

16) beef, chicken, mutton (cheese, spinach, yogurt, veal, venison)

17) oak, yew, teak (willow, dandelion, iris, beech, orchid)

18) trout, cod, salmon (whale, bream, dolphin, herring, turtle)

19) violin, guitar, cello (double bass, trumpet, tuba, viola, horn)

20) raised, aloft, higher (level, lower, above, overhead, decline)

Type S2 – two outside words connected to two inside brackets. Underline the two words inside the brackets.

e.g. Gerbil, cat (<u>hamster</u>, pet, elephant, <u>dog</u>, carpet)

They are domestic pets.

Please do the following:

1) Trout, salmon (sea, ocean, fish, herring, tuna)

2) Finger, ear (body, nose, physique, foot, cold)

3) Tulip, dandelion (rose, tree, vegetable, branch, orchid)

4) Trousers, shirt (clothes, attire, tie, uniform, jacket)

5) Uncle, aunt (grandfather, relative, ancestor, mother, pet)

6) Cheese, butter (chocolate, soup, yogurt, bacon, milkshake)

7) Happy, pleased (content, morose, disgruntled, upset, satisfied)

8) Cricket, football (rowing, tennis, archery, netball, fishing)

9) Atlantic, Arctic (Mediterranean, Indian, Pacific, Caspian, Red)

10) Mediterranean, Red (Black, Indian, Pacific, Caspian, Atlantic)

11) Severn, Trent (Snowdonia, Thames, Ben Nevis, Dee, Peak District)

12) Everest, K2 (Amazon, Kilimanjaro, Thames, Table, Pacific)

13) France, Germany (Spain, USA, Italy, Brazil, Argentina)

14) Paris, Berlin (New York, Tokyo, London, Leeds, Manchester)

15) Europe, Africa (USA, Japan, Asia, Australasia, China)

Type S3 – Two words inside the brackets have the same, or similar, meaning to the word in capitals outside the brackets. Underline the two words.

e.g. HAPPY (calm, thoughtful, <u>content</u>, decent, <u>pleased</u>)

Please do the following:

1) DISTINCT (brave, <u>original</u>, courageous, <u>unique</u>, military)

2) RECKLESS (dangerous, late, sleepless, tired, <u>careless</u>)

3) OBSTRUCTED (<u>blocked</u>, harmful, <u>delayed</u>, slow, disinterested)

4) DISASTER (<u>calamity</u>, wayward, success, <u>catastrophe</u>, tardy)

5) UNUSUAL (norm, <u>different</u>, better, standard, <u>odd</u>)

6) RUDE (<u>impolite</u>, neutral, aggressive, <u>abrupt</u>, ignorant)

7) PROHIBIT (habitual, <u>stop</u>, commence, begin, <u>ban</u>)

8) PLACID (<u>calm</u>, <u>peaceful</u>, harmful, dangerous, violent)

9) STAGNATE (suggest, <u>deteriorate</u>, improve, <u>vegetate</u>, delay)

10) RAPID (<u>quick</u>, canter, jogging, <u>fast</u>, slow)

11+ Verbal Reasoning Practice

Type S4 – There are two pairs of words. Find a word from the list that will go equally well with either pair. Write the word in the space provided.

e.g. SYMPATHETIC TYPE TREAT TONE SENSITIVE

(DELICATE, FRAGILE) (CARING, CONSIDERATE) _____ SENSITIVE _____

Please do the following:

1) (PLACID GENTLE) (SOOTHE PLACATE) _____
   CLEAR COMPARE CALM CLOSE CLAMMY

2) (TEACH LEARN) (LOCOMOTIVE DINKY) _____
   TYRE TIMBER TRAIN TIRESOME TEEMING

3) (DOMESTIC SERVANT) (ASSIST AID) _____
   ABLE HINDER HELP HOUSEMAN HOUSEMAID

4) (GAP AREA) (UNIVERSE GALAXY) _____
   EXTERNAL TIMELORD DISTANCE SOLAR SPACE

5) (THUMP WALLOP) (SUCCESSFUL POPULAR) _____
   HIT PUNCH MILESTONE STRIKE BLOW

6) (DOORWAY INGRESS) (BEWITCH HYPNOTISE) _____
   EXIT DOORFRAME ENTRANCE SPOOK WILY

7) (BOAT LINER) (SEND DISPATCH) _____
   SUBMARINE CRUISER POST SHIP COURIER

8) (EXCAVATE DIG) (OWN POSSESS) _____
   UNDERGROUND MINE BUY INHERIT GET

9) (THICK CONGESTED) (DULL STUPID) _____
   CROWDED OVER-POPULATED DENSE IGNORANT ILLITERATE

10) (CONFECTIONERY DESSERT) (NICE CUTE) _____
    SOUR PUDDING PRETTY HANDSOME SWEET

11) (DASH RUSH) (LOCK ROD) _____
    SPRINT RUN YALE BOLT MORTICE

Type U – In each question, find the letters that will complete the pair on the right hand side in the same way as the pair on the left hand side.

A B C D E F G H I J K L M N O P Q R S T U V W X Y Z

1) AB CD : GH ____

2) FD JH : KI ____

3) ZB DF : XZ ____

4) BZ EC : SQ ____

5) KL OH : I J ____

6) RO QM : KM ____

7) TR AL : WS ____

8) OJ LG : TQ ____

9) BC YF : JK ____

10) FF KA : MN ____

11) AC XF : NP ____

12) I J LO : RS ____

13) RS PP : YZ ____

14) YX AY : OP ____

15) DE HI : NO ____

16) ZY VU : PO ____

17) AC DF   :   QS _____

18) KK IH   :   OO _____

19) XX AB   :   UU _____

20) LJ KH   :   RP _____

21) WX ZA   :   XY _____

22) DC AZ   :   BA _____

23) OM KG   :   WU _____

Type Z – Read the information provided for each questions and then answer the questions which follow.

A) Five pupils in a class like some vegetables but dislike others.
Only Bill likes sprouts. Alan and Bill both like beans, as does Diane.
Surprisingly, Ellen shares Cindy's love of cabbage and everyone, of course, likes peas.

Please answer the following questions based on the information given above:

1) How many people like sprouts?

2) Which children like both peas and cabbage?

3) How many pupils like three or more vegetables?

4) Which is the least popular vegetable?

B) Alan, Bill and Charles have a number of toys between them. Alan and Bill have a total of 30. Bill and Charles have 50 between them. Together, all three have 70 toys.

1) How many toys does Alan have?

2) How many toys does Bill have?

3) How many do Alan and Charles have combined?

4) How many toys will Charles have to give to Alan so that they have the same number of toys?

C) Arif, Betty and Clara have a number of sweets between them. Arif and Betty have 38 sweets. Betty and Clara have 26 in total. Combined, the three children have a total of 54 sweets.

1) How many sweets does Betty have?

2) How many sweets does Arif have?

3) Who has the most sweets?

4) How many sweets should Arif give to Clara so that they both have the same number of sweets?

D) School starts at 08:00. Jim is always early for school.
Bill is usually early and his friend Tim gets to school before Jim sometimes.

1) Bill never gets to school before Jim.

2) Tim usually gets to school before 08:15.

3) Tim is smarter than Bill.

4) Tim gets to school before Bill sometimes.

E) Afternoons can be very hot in the summer. It can rain in the afternoon. The sun can shine for a long time during the day in summer.

1) It never rains in the morning in the summer

2) All summer days are very sunny

3) Everyone likes the summer

4) Not all summer afternoons are very hot.

F) **80% of men lose some of the hair on their heads. Some men lose all the hair on their head. 50% of men have black hair.**

1) Women never lose any hair

2) Most men are completely bald

3) One out of two men don't have black hair

4) Women like bald men

G) **All male chess players are called John. My friend's name is John. Lisa is his sister.**

1) My friend is a chess player

2) Women don't play chess

3) Lisa is older than John

4) Lisa could be a chess player

H) **James is a member of the Barnsby Swimming Club. The club meets every Tuesday and Thursday. James is very good at the backstroke. The club has many members.**

1) James likes doing the front crawl.

2) The club doesn't meet on most days of the week.

3) James is very popular at the club.

4) Today is Friday – James went to the club yesterday.

I) In four years' time, David will be 12 years old and half of his brother Bill's age. Bill was born on 1 January 1990. David was also born on 1 January.

   1) How old is David now?

   2) How old is Bill now?

   3) In which year was David born?

J) In three years' time, Jane will be three times as old as John. Jane is 33 years old now.

   1) How old is John now?

   2) What will be the difference in their ages in three years' time?

K) Tom's weight has halved over the past three years; he is now 40 Kg. Three years ago he was four times as heavy as Mary.

   1) What was Tom's weight three years ago?

   2) What was Mary's weight then?

L) Please answer the following questions:

   1) Billy's watch is 12 minutes slow. His school starts at 8.15 am. Today, Billy got to school 17 minutes late. What was the time on his watch?

   2) Tim normally catches the 8.03 am. train to Sudbury. On Monday, the train was seven minutes late. If Tim's watch is six minutes fast, what was the time on his watch when he got on the train?

3) Which month comes three months before the month which begins with the nineteenth letter of the alphabet?

4) Which month comes three months after the month which begins with the sixth letter of the alphabet?

5) Which month comes four months before the last month of the year?

6) Which month comes four months before the seventh month of the year?

7) How many months' names begin with a vowel?

8) Which day comes in the middle of the week, if Monday is the first day?

9) If tomorrow is Sunday, what was the third letter of the day before yesterday?

10) If tomorrow is Tuesday, what is the second letter of the day before yesterday?

11) A half of this number is the square of eight. What is the number?

12) Which number, when multiplied by itself, is equal to one tenth of one thousand?

13) If yesterday was Sunday, what is the third letter of the day after tomorrow?

14) In four years' time, Anne will be four times as old as Sam. Sam is now eight years old – how old is Anne now?

M) Five drivers' cars have the following features:
Emma's car has a three litre engine, as does Clare's and Brenda's. Diana's car is red as is Anna's although doesn't like it – she likes her friend Brenda's yellow car. Clare has a white car and one person has a black car.
Both Clare and Diana have a two-seater car whereas the others have four seats. All cars either have a two-litre or a three-litre engine. Both Anna and Clare's cars have leather seats whereas the rest have cloth seats.

Please answer the following questions based on the information provided above:

1) Whose has a red, four-seater car?

2) Whose car has a three-litre engine and cloth seats?

3) How many four-seater cars have cloth seats?

4) What is the most common size of engine?

N) Five pupils like a mixture of different types of reading materials.
David likes comics and non-fiction books only. Everyone except for Eric likes comics. Both Bert and Alan like science fiction – this genre of book is also Eric's favourite but Charles loathes it. Both Eric and Alan enjoy reading non-fiction books and can't understand why everyone doesn't. Charles and Alan find novels to be dull but Eric and Bert enjoy then.

Please answer the following questions based on the information provided above:

1) Who likes the fewest types of books?

2) How many pupils like two or more types of books?

3) How many pupils like both comics and science fiction?

4) Which is the most popular type of reading material?

Understanding tabulated information

Trains depart from London to Sunderland, stopping at a number of cities along the way. The express train does not stop at every station.

London	07:30	08:15	09:25	10:30
Milton Keynes	–	08:50	10:00	11:05
Birmingham	08:30	09:25	10:35	11:45
Manchester	09:35	10:40	11:50	13:00
Sunderland	11:35	12:45	13:55	15:25

Answer the following questions based on the information contained in the table above.

1) At what time does the express train depart from London?

2) Which train takes the longest to get from London to Sunderland?

3) Based on the timetable, which two consecutive cities seem to be the furthest apart?

4) If I catch the 10:00 from Milton Keynes, at what time will I get to Manchester?

5) How long does it take to get from Manchester to Sunderland if I catch the 10:30 from London?

6) If I catch the 07:30 from London, how much quicker is my journey from Manchester to Sunderland than that in Question (5) above?

7) How many trains get to Sunderland before 13:30?

8) What is the latest train I can catch from Milton Keynes if I have to be in Sunderland before 14:00?

Change a letter in the first word and write a valid word in the space provided.

e.g. L A M E __LANE_____ L I N E (LIME would also be correct)

1) B A S E _____ C A S T

2) T O R T _____ P O U T

3) M I C E _____ L A C E

4) M A L L _____ H A L E

5) P A I L _____ L A I R

6) H I N D _____ B O N D

7) T R I P _____ G R I T

8) P O L E _____ T I L E

9) P A R K _____ P A N T

10) S I N K _____ S O N G

11) M I N E _____ P A N E

12) S O M E _____ S A V E

13) T Y R E _____ P O R E

14) Y O U R _____ P O U T

15) M I R E _____ N I L E

16) M O R E _____ M A Z E

17) M E R E _____ D I R E

18) S E A R _____ N E A T

19) G R I T _____ G A I N

20) L O N E _____ B O R E

21) T U R N _____ B A R N

22) S A N E _____ S O M E

23) Z E A L _____ M E A N

Anagrams

1) L I R P A   Month of the year

2) W E E T V L   A factor of 96

3) E E E N V L   The fifth prime number

4) M E T E S R E P B Month of the year

5) G E T I H   A half of a quarter of 64

6) D R H N D E U   Square of 10

7) E E T R H T N I   A factor of 91

8) U F R O   Square of the first prime number

9) E S D R I L O   Marches on parade

10) B A U F Y R R E   Month of the year

11) D O A R S   Cars drive on these

12) C I P C A I F   An ocean

13) R M H C A   Month of the year

14) R A M U N E S I B   Underwater vessel

15) A R T N I   Locomotive is another word for it

16) D D E S W N Y E A   Day of the week

17) D M P E O   A type of motorbike

18) B L W O E   A joint in the body

19) N U S A Y D   Day of the week

20) S C I P M Y L O   Sporting event held every leap year

21) Y N A A J R U   Month of the year

22) M H O S T C A   A part of the body

23) U T Y A S A D R   Day of the week

24) N I N T E S   Wimbledon is famous for this

25) E G R I F N   Part of a hand

26) W E N O R K Y   King Kong visited this city!

27) S R Y T A D U H   Day of the week

28) O N Y H E   Bees make this

29) U U A G T S   Month of the year

30) H C T S E   Part of the upper body

31) D I A R R O A T   Part of the central heating system

32) R V N B O E E M   Month of the year

33) L L O F B T A O   A popular sport

34) U P L S P I   The majority of a school's population

35) B T O R C O E   Month of the year

36) S I L A C U M   A type of play or film

37) B M D R E E E C   Month of the year

38) S K E E H C   A part of your face

39) Y D M N A O   Day of the week

40) I A H R   Bald men wish they had more of this

41) U S T A E Y D   Day of the week

42) P I L I T S K C   A cosmetic used on the lips

What is in the middle according to size or type?

e.g. seven, ten, sixteen, <u>fifteen</u>, eighteen

1) Oil tanker, dinghy, canoe, tug, cruise liner

2) Snail, whale, dog, cat, mouse

3) Football, table-tennis ball, basketball, golf ball, tennis ball

4) 10p, 50p, £2, £1, 7p

5) 17, 33, 35, 12, 9

6) Man, baby, adolescent, toddler, pensioner

7) Jumbo jet, kite, fighter plane, glider, paper plane

8) 2 m, 500 mm, 55 cm, 0.51 m, 1 m

9) Galaxy, Moon, Sun, Earth, Jupiter

10) ½, 0.33, ⅛, ¼, 0.1

11) £1.25, £2.25, 220p, 127p, 99p

12) Car, lorry, bike, skateboard, roller-skates

13) Pin, sewing needle, javelin, arrow, dart

14) Fingernail, finger, arm, hand, body

15) Toe, foot, leg, toenail, body

16) Alan, Stanislav, Wendy, Thomas, Valentina

17) Bedroom, mansion, castle, small flat, house

18) Brook, ocean, stream, river, sea

19) 0.70, 0.94, 0.88, 0.76, 0.71

20) Continent, village, county, country, town

Three-letter word crosswords.

O	N	E

ONE NET WET
SOW SON

	A	
	P	
	E	

TAB APE BET
GET TAG

	A	
	R	
	E	

PET ARE MAP
MAN NET

	U	
	S	
	E	

TEA PEA USE
PUP PUT

	E	
	R	
	A	

TAR ERA WAR
YET YEW

I	R	E

VET ERA TER
VIE EAR

B	E	T

NEW EWE WET
NAB AWE

T	E	E

ATE EAT TEA
ERE EAR

R	E	N

TER TAB ERA
ARE BAN

	E	
	R	
	E	

ZEN PEW NEW
ZAP ARE

I	R	E

BAN NET ARE
BET BIB

T	E	A

IRE TEA ARE
HIT HAT

		T
		E
		N

TEN FOE ROE
ART AFT

		P
		E
		N

SIP IRE TEN
ARE SAT

L	E	E

NEE LET NET
INN ILL

Y	E	T

AYE LYE PLY
YET PAY

Underline the two words within the brackets which can't be made from the word in CAPITALS.

1) INCREDULOUS   (soul, dinner, solid, cruel, clever)

2) INCONGRUOUS   (brain, grin, soon, gross, noun)

3) TREMENDOUS   (dent, mentor, dire, your, rent)

4) IRRESPONSIBLE   (pose, sole, response, terrible, present)

5) MILITANCY   (tail, mint, tall, train, mail)

6) CONSIDERATE   (constant, cider, react, daring, drone)

7) INGRATIATE   (grate, green, trail, grain, target)

8) SPINELESS   (pine, less, plan, spell, spin)

9) LABORIOUS   (slur, riot, sour, slab, sale)

10) RESPECTABLE   (tablet, spore, stable, pest, create)

11) TECHNOLOGICAL   (aching, notch, logistics, calendar, change)

12) SEISMOLOGICAL   (local, molar, slice, lane, goal)

13) TENACIOUS   (scent, seat, paint, stone, curious)

14) PERAMBULATOR   (ramble, tumble, butter, ramrod, lame)

15) SPENDTHRIFT   (fret, trend, speed, right, pins)

16) INSTALLATION   (talent, station, instant, stable, stall)

17) GRAVITATE   (rave, vital, tiger, grate, train)

18) GLADIATOR   (loud, load, riot, trout, toad)

19) SURREPTITIOUS   (surprise, tire, pray, pleasure, trip)

20) OCEANOLOGY   (goal, clean, cone, logic, yearn)

A) The following words have to be spelled backwards and then put in alphabetical order (e.g. BAIT becomes TIAB):

Disable, Dependable, Incredible, Reliable, Contestable

Now answer the following questions:

1) Which word would come second?

2) Which word would come fourth?

3) Which word would come third?

B) The following words have to be written backwards and then put in alphabetical order (e.g. BAIT becomes TIAB):

Bubble, Trouble, Double, Noble, Constable

Now answer the following questions:

1) Which word would come second?

2) Which word would come fourth?

3) Which word would come third?

C) The following words have to be written backwards and then put in alphabetical order (e.g. BAIT becomes TIAB):

Staid, Paid, Maid, Braid, Laid

Now answer the following questions:

1) Which word would come second?

2) Which word would come fourth?

3) Which word would come third?

D) Please answer the following questions:

1) Make a word from the letters which appear more than once in **I T E R A T I O N**

2) Make a word from the letters which appear more than once in **L A S S O O**

3) Make a word from the letters which appear more than once in **A T T A C K**

Related words have been grouped together in the table below – they have been labelled A, B, C, D and E. Beneath the table there are nine words – decide which group they belong to and write the letter A, B, C, D and E in the space next to the word.

A	B	C	D	E
Yew	Sparrow	Argentina	Paris	Dee
Oak	Starling	France	Rome	Severn
Willow	Canary	Spain	Washington DC	Thames

1) Italy ____   4) Madrid ____   7) Danube ____

2) Rhine ____   5) Brussels ____   8) Egypt ____

3) Teak ____   6) Robin ____   9) Poplar ____

A	B	C	D	E
Football	Mediterranean	Everest	Guitar	Belgium
Cricket	Black	Eiger	Violin	USA
Hockey	Caspian	Kilimanjaro	Piano	Mexico

1) Brazil ____   4) Lacrosse ____   7) Japan ____

2) K2 ____   5) Everest ____   8) Baltic ____

3) Cello ____   6) North ____   9) Rugby ____

A	B	C	D	E
Montevideo	Vesuvius	Shannon	Croatia	Atlantic
Tokyo	Etna	Amazon	Germany	Arctic
London	St Helens	Thames	Holland	Indian

1) Pacific ____   4) Wales ____   7) Berlin ____

2) Paris ____   5) Krakatau ____   8) Lisbon ____

3) Yangtze ____   6) Seine ____   9) Greece ____

A	B	C	D	E
Redwood	Spain	Football	Tulip	Nile
Oak	Italy	Tennis	Rose	Rhine
Elm	Uruguay	Basketball	Orchid	Seine

1) Ganges ____   4) Mongolia ____   7) Polo ____

2) Beech ____   5) Dee ____   8) Tanzania ____

3) Iris ____   6) Shannon ____   9) Poplar ____

A	B	C	D	E
Russian	Paris	Copper	Thames	Wales
Spanish	London	Lead	Amazon	France
English	Moscow	Silver	Seine	Belgium

1) Namibia ____   4) Volga ____   7) Libya ____

2) Gold ____   5) Berlin ____   8) Zinc ____

3) Mandarin ____   6) Portuguese ____   9) Danube ____

Numbers missing from calculations – write the missing numbers in place of the asterisks (*).

1)   1 3 7
   + * 7 *
   ─────
     6 * 2

2)   5 * *
   + * 6 8
   ─────
   1 3 3 5

3)   * 5 *
   + 4 * 6
   ─────
     9 3 1

4)   * 9 9
   + 2 * *
   ─────
   1 2 9 8

5)   6 * 7
     * 6 *
   ─────
     9 2 1

6)   3 4 5
   + * * *
   ─────
     5 1 0

7)   * * *
   + 2 3 4
   ─────
     6 9 0

8)   7 * 8
   + * 2 *
   ─────
     9 4 1

9)   * 9 8
   + 3 * *
   ─────
     9 4 3

10) 7 * 7
   + * 4 *
   ─────
   1 2 1 2

11) * * *
   + 6 5 4
   ─────
   1 2 2 2

12) 9 8 7
   + * * *
   ─────
   1 5 1 0

13) 9 8 7
   − * * 3
   ─────
     1 6 *

14) 5 4 3
   − 3 3 4
   ─────
     * * *

15) 6 * *
   − * 7 4
   ─────
     5 1 9

16) 4 * 8
   − * 5 *
   ─────
     1 9 1

17) * 6 3
   − 5 * *
   ─────
     2 8 0

18) 7 8 1
   − * * *
   ─────
     4 3 2

19) 5 * 9
   − * 4 3
   ─────
     2 9 *

20) * * 4
   − 5 6 *
   ─────
     3 2 7

Underline the appropriate words inside the brackets that will make a sensible sentence.

1) The brilliant (butcher / architect / doctor) put his (stethoscope / paper / comb) on the boy's (fish / chest / glasses).

2) The busy (dentist / teacher / fishmonger) quickly (mocked / marked / mashed) the pile of (housework / oven / homework).

3) The brave (astronaut / clown / witch) climbed into the (train / boat / spaceship) to go to the (bathroom / Moon / supermarket).

4) Early morning, the (butcher / baker / candlestick maker) prepared the (door / dour / dough) before putting it into the (fryer / oven / fridge).

5) The experienced (dancer / singer / soldier) loaded the (bullet / ballet / ballot) into the (rifle / tutu / microphone).

6) You have to mix (flower / flour / floor) with the (batter / bother / butter) when baking a (coke / cup / cake).

7) When swimming (underwater / in a street / in a shop) you need (water / soil / air) in a tank to (breathe / breath / width).

8) You should answer your (TV / phone / radio) when it (sings / pings / rings) because someone is (calling / pulling / hitting) you.

9) If you add (two / three / seven) to (fifteen / sixteen / seventeen) you get (twenty / thirty / forty) as an answer.

10) If you add (seven / eight / nine) to (twelve / thirteen / fourteen) you get (nineteen / twenty four / twenty seven) as the answer.

11) If you subtract (five / six / seven) from (twenty / nineteen / twenty one) you get (twelve / eight / seven) as the answer.

12) You have to put (soap / shampoo/ toothpaste) on your (stick / brush / flannel) to brush your (hair / moustache/ teeth).

13) (Cricket / hockey / badminton) is played with (rackets / sticks / bats) and (dice / coins / shuttlecocks).

14) You use a (knife / pen / spoon) to (spray / write / spread) on (carpets / wood / paper).

68   11+ Verbal Reasoning Practice

A B C D E F G H I J K L M N O P Q R S T U V W X Y Z

Use the alphabet above to help work out which two letters come next in the following sequences.

e.g. AB BC CD DE EF ___FG___ ___GH___

The sequence, in this case, is reading the alphabet forwards for both letters.

Please do the following:

1) NT PQ SO UL XJ _____

2) GG HC JY MV QT _____

3) EP BN HN EL KL _____

4) AJ BM CP DS EV _____

5) AB PY ZC OX YD _____

6) DA EZ GX JU NQ _____

7) MN LO KP JQ IR _____

8) XW ZT CQ GN LK _____

9) PX QV SU TS _____

10) BP DU AQ CV ZR _____

11) CM GS IX MB OE _____

12) DM WN EL VO FK _____

13) CE FJ LO UT GY _____

14) BB CD EF GH KJ _____

15) AK CL DJ FM GI _____

16) MA ZZ AY NX AW _____

VR Exercises

11 Plus Verbal Reasoning Answers

Copyright of Great Tutors. All rights reserved. No part of this publication may be reproduced or transmitted in any form or by any means, electronic or mechanical, including photocopying, recording or duplication in any information storage and retrieval system.

Page 2

1) E	7) E	13) T	19) N
2) L	8) F	14) R	20) T
3) A	9) K	15) L	21) Y
4) P	10) L	16) E	22) B
5) H	11) S	17) T	23) D
6) D	12) S	18) R	24) P

Pages 3 and 4

1) Dame	7) Earl	13) Nine	19) Sixteen	25) A (vowel)
2) Eight	8) Victoria	14) Atlantic	20) Diamond	
3) USA	9) Seasons	15) Eerie	21) Nose	
4) North	10) Calendar	16) Torso	22) House	
5) Four	11) Fifteen	17) Fifteen	23) Horse	
6) Birmingham	12) Rhine	18) Thomas	24) Four	

Pages 5 and 6

1) Countess, Dame	6) Time, Measurement	11) Warsaw, Berlin	16) Justin Bieber, Michael Bublé
2) Baron, Earl	7) Piano, Violin	12) Leeds, Nice	17) Five, Eleven
3) Sun, Universe	8) Serengeti, Yosemite	13) Brass, Diamante	18) Seal, Madonna
4) Monkey, Ape	9) Four, Six	14) Walking, Running	19) Five, Seven
5) Hockey, Swimming	10) Argentina, Brazil	15) Two, Twelve	20) Anxious, Morose

Pages 7 and 8

1) Rest (2) Voice (3) Pasta (4) Kiss (5) Table (6) QDVB (7) RTFDO (8) WRZHU
(9) 4, 1, 14, 7, 5, 18 (10) G J J E I U (11) 6, 3, 10, 14 (12) U Q V R U (13) 22, 20, 3, 11, 14
(14) 20, 8, 13, 8, 4 (15) F, 17, P, 21, C (16) M, M, E, E, F (17) Train (18) Moan
(19) Zebra (20) Toast

Pages 9, 10, 11 and 12

1) @ + & + \
2) @ + # −
3) & − & + \
4) & ! + \ ! ! & \
5) @ # − @ + = + # + \
6) + ! # − @
7) ! = # @ $
8) ! # − + & !
9) ! & + # ! @
10) + ! = \ − @ $
11) Tramps
12) Trumpet
13) Repeat
14) Streets
15) Premature
16) Drones
17) Mended
18) Demons
19) Modern
20) Trust
21) H G F M
22) K V M W
23) K V M G
24) H L F K
25) W V M G
26) M V H G
27) M L H V
28) G L M V
29) E V H G
30) C D N G
31) D C N G
32) O C N G
33) D G C O
34) I L S B
35) O L S B
36) I L A B
37) Z L S B
38) T V B P E
39) V G P E
40) T B P E
41) E B P D G
42) T V B P D G

Pages 13 and 14

1) happy, content
2) tired, fatigued
3) assertive, forceful
4) clever, intelligent
5) considerate, thoughtful
6) hindrance, obstruction
7) placid, calm
8) dogged, determined
9) comprehend, understand
10) broad, wide
11) indolent, lazy
12) increase, gain
13) ingest, swallow
14) consume, eat
15) chat, converse
16) fascinated, riveted
17) discord, disagreement
18) trivial, unimportant
19) mundane, boring
20) unusual, odd
21) tangible, real
22) belief, faith

Pages 15 and 16

1) than
2) inch (or meat)
3) edge
4) wood
5) shed
6) wove
7) tone
8) wand
9) form
10) onus (or soft)
11) tape
12) reed
13) this
14) very
15) rear
16) tyre
17) bard
18) tent
19) real
20) isle (or none)

Pages 17 and 18

1) WAY
2) NET
3) DIN
4) OAT
5) ARK
6) TAR
7) LIE
8) ARE or EAR
9) OLD
10) ONE
11) BAN
12) ARE
13) HAM
14) AIR
15) ANT
16) TIN
17) PUT
18) IMP
19) OLD
20) RID
21) ROW

Pages 19 and 20

1) 8
2) A
3) E
4) 3
5) D
6) B
7) 20
8) B
9) A
10) A
11) D
12) 1
13) 5
14) C
15) 5
16) B
17) 6.5
18) 70
19) 0
20) E

Pages 21 and 22

1) happy, sad
2) placid, flustered
3) fat, thin
4) tall, short
5) dark, light
6) evening, morning
7) content, unhappy
8) old, young
9) light, heavy
10) flexible, rigid
11) energetic, lethargic
12) tense, slack
13) quiet, loud
14) clear, hazy
15) soften, harden
16) boiling, freezing
17) increased, reduced
18) frowning, smiling
19) declined, accepted
20) introvert, extrovert
21) charming, obnoxious

Pages 23 and 24

1) (20 ÷ 4 + 7)
2) (6 X 3 − 5) or (3 X 6 − 5)
3) (6 + 4 ÷ 2)
4) (10 ÷ 2 X 3)
5) (8 X 9 − 7) or (9 X 8 − 7)
6) (40 ÷ 2 − 3)
7) (81 ÷ 3 − 7)
8) (9 + 8 − 1) or (8 + 9 − 1)
9) (10 + 7 + 6) any order is ok
10) (12 X 5 + 6) or (5 X 12 + 6)
11) (9 X 3 − 4) or (3 X 9 − 4)
12) (6 ÷ 3 + 5)
13) (6 + 10 X 8) or (6 + 10 X 8)
14) (11 − 8 − 2)
15) (13 X 7 + 12) or (7 X 13 + 12)
16) (6 ÷ 3 X 5)
17) (9 ÷ 3 X 7)
18) (8 − 4 X 7)
19) (13 X 5 + 3) or (5 X 13 + 3) or (11 x 5 + 13)
20) (8 ÷ 4 X 7)

Page 25

1) leer and halve
2) pace and stool
3) cod and melt
4) mid and kiln
5) bran and anti
6) ale and brain
7) cob and moat
8) art and dice
9) cow and barn
10) mat and nest
11) sow and part (or tow, spar)
12) rap and peer
13) hate and strap
14) hose and pout
15) rash and witch
16) rat and pale
17) done and cart
18) tint and wait
19) doe and plane
20) mat and load

Pages 26 and 27

(1) **5** (2 x 5 − 5) 2B − A
(2) **33** (2 x 12 + 9) 2A + B
(3) **18** [(8 + 28) / 2]
(4) **31** (13 + 3 x 6) A + 3B
(5) **104** (100^2 + 4) A^2 + B
(6) **18** (7 + 22 ÷ 2) A + B ÷ 2
(7) **17** (9 + $\sqrt{64}$) A + $\sqrt{B}$
(8) **64** [2 (11 + 21)] 2(A + B)
(9) **8** (72 ÷ 9) A ÷ B
(10) **20** (2 x 13 − 6) 2A − B
(11) **52** [(100 + 4) ÷ 2] (A + B) ÷ 2
(12) **84** (10^2 − 2 x 8) A^2 − 2B
(13) **30** (4 + 2 x 13) A + 2B
(14) **2** [(2 x 9) ÷ 9] 2A ÷ B
(15) **78** (14 + 8^2) A + B^2
(16) **12** (30 − 3 x 6) A − 3B
(17) **33** (17 + 6 + 10) A + B + 10
(18) **11** (2 x 9 − 7) 2B − A
(19) **12** [(20 + 4) ÷ 2] (A + B) ÷ 2
(20) **41** (5 + 6^2) A + B^2

Page 28

1) K M (+ 2)
2) K H (– 3)
3) R P (– 2)
4) X E (+2, +3, +4 +5, +6, +7)
5) V O (––2, –3, –4 –5, –6, –7)
6) Q P (+2, –1)
7) D I (+5)
8) E T (+1, –3, +5, –7, +9, –11)
9) V G (–1, +3, –5, +7, –9, +11)
10) P V (+1, +2, +3, +4)
11) K E (–1, –2, –3, –4)
12) N K (+5, –3)
13) N P (–5, +2)
14) Z V (+2, –4)
15) X T (+3, –4)
16) R T (+3, +2, +4, +2, +5, +2)
17) G E (–4, –2)
18) M U (+1, +1, +2, +3, +5, +8...Fibonacci)

Pages 29 and 30

1) car, plane
2) window, bed
3) floor, meadow
4) gun, bow
5) milk, wheat
6) cow, pig
7) sheep, goat
8) cricket, hockey
9) sea, sky
10) land, water
11) rail, road
12) fuel, food
13) South America, Africa
14) mountain range, ocean
15) words, arithmetic
16) meat, vegetables
17) metal, stone
18) country, city
19) tooth, eye
20) temperature, length
21) East, West
22) three, five
23) agricultural, industrial

Pages 31 and 32

1) 1 2 4 5 3 1
2) 2 3 8 4 8 5 3
3) C A N E S
4) P A N I C S
5) 4 7 2 5
6) 4 2 9 8
7) 8 7 3 3
8) S I R E
9) 3 6 7 8
10) 8 7 3 6
11) R O P E
12) A R E A
13) 2 4 6 3
14) 2 5 6 4
15) S E E N
16) T E N D
17) 1 4 2 3
18) 3 5 6 4
19) S A M E
20) S E A T
21) 6 1 3 5
22) 4 5 1 3
23) T E A S E
24) T R E E S

Page 33

1) earl (remove 1st letter)
2) wish (remove 1st letter)
3) pal (remove 3rd letter)
4) beet (remove 1st two letters and replace with B)
5) pan (remove 3rd letter)
6) own (remove 1st letter)
7) pecks (move 1st letter to end)
8) pater (insert T into middle and switch last two letters)
9) tone (add E to the 1st three letters)
10) sat (remove 2nd and 4th letters)
11) rut (remove 1st two letters)
12) man (move the 4th letter in front of 2nd & 3rd)
13) past (4th letter substituted with next in alphabet)
14) to (1st and last letters only)
15) slay (1st two letters plus 'ay')
16) got (1st, 3rd and 4th letters only)
17) grin (remove 3rd letter)
18) knee (1st two letters plus last letter plus E)

Pages 34 and 35

1) 9 (+2)
2) 32 (X 2)
3) 120 (÷ 2)
4) 27 (X 3)
5) 3 (3+5=8, 5+8=13, 8+13=21)
6) 16 (square numbers)
16) 100 (alternating sequence ... 25, 5, 1 and 100, 500, 2500)
17) 16 (increasing gap between numbers ... +1, +2, +3 etc.)
18) 21 (increasing gap between numbers ... –1, –2, –3 etc.)
19) 6 (alternating sequence ... 3, 4, 5 and 5, 6, 7)
20) 99 (alternating sequence...99, 98, 97 and 97, 96, 95)
21) 16 (X 4)

11 Plus Verbal Reasoning Answers

7) 8.5 (+ 1.5)
8) 4 (+ 0.25)
9) 12.20 (− 0.5)
10) 100 (descending square numbers)
11) −5 (−3, −4, −5, −6)
12) 51 (−5, −6, −7, −8)
13) 729 (X 3)
14) 25 (+3, −4, +3, −4)
15) 80 (−20, +10, −20, +10)

22) 125 (÷ 5)
23) 2 (− 3)
24) −11 (increasing gap between numbers ... 2, 3, 4 etc.)
25) −1.3 (+ 0.3)
26) −11.5 (+ 0.25)
27) 750 (− 150)
28) 54 (X 3)
29) 2 (÷ 3)
30) 1175 (−125, −25, −125....)

Page 36

1) bee, hive
2) car, pet
3) foot, ball
4) hand, some
5) in, let
6) pat, tern
7) lab, our
8) can, did
9) bat, on
10) mouse, trap
11) over, turn
12) sea, son
13) cross, bow
14) sun, burn
15) net, ball
16) goal, post
17) orb, it
18) farm, hand
19) ab, cess
20) be, little

Pages 37 and 38

1) bait
2) away
3) pest
4) mean
5) neat
6) pelt
7) sate
8) tone (or tome)
9) pare
10) goal
11) bone (or bond)
12) pole
13) damp
14) time
15) coat (or coal)
16) bear
17) scar
18) prop
19) send
20) sear
21) late
22) draw
23) mild

Page 39

1) gold, platinum
2) second, hour
3) football, netball
4) Rome, Moscow
5) Italy, Romania
6) Volga, Rhine
7) Yorkshire, Lancashire
8) Leicester, Loughborough (all start with 'L')
9) K2, Matterhorn
10) two, eleven (prime numbers)
11) trumpet, flute (brass instruments)
12) four, one (square numbers)
13) iris, petunia
14) wasp, locust
15) parallelogram, trapezium
16) veal, venison
17) willow, beech
18) bream, herring
19) double bass, viola (string instruments)
20) above, overhead

Page 40
1) herring, tuna
2) nose, foot
3) rose, orchid
4) tie, jacket
5) grandfather, mother
6) yogurt, milkshake
7) content, satisfied
8) tennis, netball
9) Indian, Pacific
10) Black, Caspian
11) Thames, Dee
12) Kilimanjaro, Table
13) Spain, Italy
14) Tokyo, London
15) Asia, Australasia

Page 41
1) original, unique
2) dangerous, careless
3) blocked, delayed
4) calamity, catastrophe
5) different, odd
6) impolite, abrupt
7) stop, ban
8) calm, peaceful
9) deteriorate, vegetate
10) quick, fast

Page 42
1) calm
2) train
3) help
4) space
5) hit
6) entrance
7) ship
8) mine
9) dense
10) sweet
11) bolt

Pages 43 and 44
1) I J
2) O M
3) B D
4) V T
5) M F
6) J K
7) D M
8) Q N
9) G N
10) R I
11) K S
12) U X
13) W W
14) Q Q
15) R S
16) L K
17) T V
18) M L
19) X Y
20) Q N
21) A B
22) Y X
23) S O

Page 45 and 46
A1) 1
A2) Cindy, Ellen
A3) 1
A4) Sprouts
B1) 20
B2) 10
B3) 40
B4) 10
C1) 10
C2) 28
C3) Arif
C4) 6

Pages 46 and 47
D) 4   F) 3
E) 4   G) 4

Pages 47 and 48
H) 2
I1) 8   I2) 20   I3) 2002
J1) 9   J2) 24
K1) 80 K2) 20

11 Plus Verbal Reasoning Answers

Pages 48 and 49
L1) 8.20 am   L5) August   L9) U   L13) D
L2) 8.16 am   L6) March   L10) A   L14) 44 years
L3) June   L7) 3   L11) 128
L4) May   L8) Thursday L12) 10

Page 50
M1) Anna   N1) Charles
M2) Brenda   N2) 4
M3) 2   N3) 2
M4) 3 litre N4) Comics

Page 51
1) 7.30
2) 10.30
3) Manchester & Sunderland
4) 11.50
5) 2 hours and 25 minutes
6) 25 minutes
7) 2
8) 10.00

Pages 52 and 53
1) CASE   2) PORT/TOUT   3) LICE   4) HALL /MALE
5) PAIR   6) BIND   7) GRIP   8) PILE
9) PART   10) SING   11) PINE/MANE   12) SAME
13) TORE/PYRE 14) POUR   15) MILE   16) MARE
17) MIRE   18) NEAR/SEAT   19) GRIN/GAIT   20) BONE/LORE
21) BURN   22) SAME   23) MEAL

Pages 54, 55 and 56
1) APRIL   2) TWELVE   3) ELEVEN   4) SEPTEMBER
5) EIGHT   6) HUNDRED   7) THIRTEEN   8) FOUR
9) SOLDIER   10) FEBRUARY   11) ROADS   12) PACIFIC
13) MARCH   14) SUBMARINE   15) TRAIN   16) WEDNESDAY
17) MOPED   18) ELBOW   19) SUNDAY   20) OLYMPICS
21) JANUARY   22) STOMACH   23) SATURDAY   24) TENNIS
25) FINGER   26) NEW YORK   27) THURSDAY   28) HONEY
29) AUGUST   30) CHEST   31) RADIATOR   32) NOVEMBER
33) FOOTBALL   34) PUPILS   35) OCTOBER   36) MUSICAL
37) DECEMBER   38) CHEEKS   39) MONDAY   40) HAIR
41) TUESDAY   42) LIPSTICK

Pages 57 and 58
1) tug   2) cat   3) tennis ball   4) 50p
5) 17   6) adolescent   7) glider   8) 55 cm
9) Jupiter   10) ¼   11) 127p   12) bike
13) dart   14) hand   15) foot   16) Thomas
17) house   18) river   19) 0.76   20) county

76   11+ Verbal Reasoning Practice

Pages 59 and 60

Three-letter word crosswords.

S	O	N
O	N	E
W	E	T

ONE NET WET
SOW SON

T	A	B
A	P	E
G	E	T

TAB APE BET
GET TAG

M	A	P
A	R	E
N	E	T

PET ARE MAP
MAN NET

P	U	P
U	S	E
T	E	A

TEA PEA USE
PUP PUT

Y	E	W
E	R	A
T	A	R

TAR ERA WAR
YET YEW

V	E	T
I	R	E
E	R	A

VET ERA TER
VIE EAR

N	E	W
A	W	E
B	E	T

NEW EWE WET
NAB AWE

T	E	E
E	A	R
A	T	E

ATE EAT TEA
ERE EAR

T	A	B
E	R	A
R	E	N

TER TAB ERA
ARE BAN

Z	E	N
A	R	E
P	E	W

ZEN PEW NEW
ZAP ARE

B	A	N
I	R	E
B	E	T

BAN NET ARE
BET BIB

H	I	T
A	R	E
T	E	A

IRE TEA ARE
HIT HAT

A	R	T
F	O	E
T	E	N

TEN FOE ROE
ART AFT

S	I	P
A	R	E
T	E	N

SIP IRE TEN
ARE SAT

I	N	N
L	E	E
L	E	T

NEE LET NET
INN ILL

P	L	Y
A	Y	E
Y	E	T

AYE LYE PLY
YET PAY

Page 61
1) dinner, clever
2) brain, gross
3) dire, your
4) terrible, present
5) tall, train
6) constant, daring
7) green, trail
8) plan, spell
9) riot, sale
10) tablet, spore
11) logistics, calendar
12) molar, lane
13) paint, curious
14) butter, ramrod
15) speed, right
16) talent, stable
17) vital, train
18) loud, trout
19) pray, pleasure
20) logic, yearn

Page 62
A1) reliable
A2) contestable
A3) disable
B1) bubble
B2) double
B3) noble
C1) maid
C2) braid
C3) paid

Page 63
1) it
2) so
3) at

78   11+ Verbal Reasoning Practice

Pages 64 and 65

A	B	C	D	E
Yew	Sparrow	Argentina	Paris	Dee
Oak	Starling	France	Rome	Severn
Willow	Canary	Spain	Washington DC	Thames

1) Italy _C__   4) Madrid __D__   7) Danube _E__
2) Rhine __E__   5) Brussels __D__   8) Egypt _C__
3) Teak __A__   6) Robin _B__   9) Poplar __A__

A	B	C	D	E
Football	Mediterranean	Everest	Guitar	Belgium
Cricket	Black	Eiger	Violin	USA
Hockey	Caspian	Kilimanjaro	Piano	Mexico

1) Brazil _E___   4) Lacrosse _A___   7) Japan __E__
2) K2 _C__   5) Everest __C__   8) Baltic __B__
3) Cello __D__   6) North __B__   9) Rugby __A__

A	B	C	D	E
Montevideo	Vesuvius	Shannon	Croatia	Atlantic
Tokyo	Etna	Amazon	Germany	Arctic
London	St Helens	Thames	Holland	Indian

1) Pacific ___E__   4) Wales __D__   7) Berlin __A___
2) Paris __A__   5) Krakatau __B__   8) Lisbon __A___
3) Yangtze __C___   6) Seine __C___   9) Greece __D___

Page 57

A	B	C	D	E
Redwood	Spain	Football	Tulip	Nile
Oak	Italy	Tennis	Rose	Rhine
Elm	Uruguay	Basketball	Orchid	Seine

(1) Ganges _E__   (4) Mongolia __B__   (7) Polo __C__
(2) Beech __A__   (5) Dee __E__   (8) Tanzania __B__
(3) Iris _D___   (6) Shannon __E__   (9) Poplar __A__

A	B	C	D	E
Russian	Paris	Copper	Thames	Wales
Spanish	London	Lead	Amazon	France
English	Moscow	Silver	Seine	Belgium

(1) Namibia _E__   (4) Volga _D__   (7) Libya __E__
(2) Gold __C__   (5) Berlin __B_   (8) Zinc __C__
(3) Mandarin __A__ (6) Portuguese _A__ (9) Danube __D__

Page 66

1) 1 3 7   2) 5 6 7   3) 4 5 5   4) 9 9 9   5) 6 5 7
   +4 7 5   +7 6 8   +4 7 6   +2 9 9   +2 6 4
    6 1 2   1 3 3 5   9 3 1   1 2 9 8   9 2 1

6) 3 4 5   7) 4 5 6   8) 7 1 8   9) 5 9 8   10) 7 6 7
   +1 6 5   +2 3 4   +2 2 3   +3 4 5   +4 4 5
    5 1 0   6 9 0   9 4 1   9 4 3   1 2 1 2

11) 5 6 8   12) 9 8 7
   +6 5 4   +5 2 3
  1 2 2 2   1 5 1 0

13) 9 8 7   14) 5 4 3   15) 6 9 3   16) 4 4 8   17) 8 6 3
   -8 2 3   -3 3 4   -1 7 4   -2 5 7   -5 8 3
    1 6 4   2 0 9   5 1 9   1 9 1   2 8 0

18) 7 8 1   19) 5 3 9   20) 8 9 4
   -3 4 9   -2 4 3   -5 6 7
    4 3 2   2 9 6   3 2 7

Page 67

1) doctor, stethoscope, chest   4) baker, dough, oven   7) underwater, air, breathe
2) teacher, marked, homework   5) soldier, bullet, rifle   8) phone, rings, calling
3) astronaut, spaceship, Moon   6) flour, butter, cake   9) three, seventeen, twenty
10) seven, twelve, nineteen   11) seven, nineteen, twelve   12) toothpaste, brush, teeth
13) badminton, rackets, shuttlecocks   14) pen, write, paper

Page 68

1) ZG   (2) VS   (3) HJ   (4) FY   (5) NW   (6) SL   (7) HS   (8) RH   (9) VR
10) BW   (11) SG   (12) UP   (13) VD   (14) QN   (15) IN   (16) BV